YOU CAN DO IT!

Football

Kirk Bizley

Heinemann
LIBRARY

To Jake

First published in Great Britain by Heinemann Library
Halley Court, Jordan Hill, Oxford OX2 8EJ
a division of Reed Educational and Professional Publishing Ltd.
Heinemann is a registered trademark of Reed Educational & Professional Publishing Limited.

OXFORD MELBOURNE AUCKLAND IBADAN JOHANNESBURG
BLANTYRE GABORONE PORTSMOUTH (NH) USA CHICAGO

Designed by Ken Vail Graphic Design, Cambridge
Illustrations by Graham-Cameron Illustration (Tony O'Donnell)
Originated by Ambassador Litho Ltd
Printed by Wing King Tong in Hong Kong

04 03
10 9 8 7 6 5 4 3 2

ISBN 0 431 08533 1
This title is also available in a hardback library edition (ISBN 0 431 08532 3)

British Library Cataloguing in Publication Data

Bizley, Kirk
Football. – (You can do it)
1. Soccer – Juvenile literature
I. Title
796.3'34

Acknowledgements
The author would like to thank the staff and pupils of Shepton Mallett Community Infants School.

The Publishers would like to thank the following for permission to reproduce photographs:
Allsport, page 20 (bottom) /Shaun Botterill; Gareth Boden, page 6 (bottom); Trevor Clifford pages 4,
5, 8, 10, 11, 12, 13, 14, 16, 17, 20 (top); Empics, page 6 (top) /Matthew Ashton, 18.

Cover photograph reproduced with permission of Tony Stone Images /Lori Adamski Peck.

Our thanks to Betty Root for her comments in the preparation of this book.

Every effort has been made to contact copyright holders of any material reproduced in this book.
Any omissions will be rectified in subsequent printings if notice is given to the Publisher.

For more information about Heinemann Library books, or to order, please phone 01865 888066,
or send a fax to 01865 314091. You can visit our web site at www.heinemann.co.uk

Contents

Words in bold letters **like these** are explained in the Glossary.

What do you need?

To play football you need a T-shirt, shorts, socks and shoes or boots to wear.

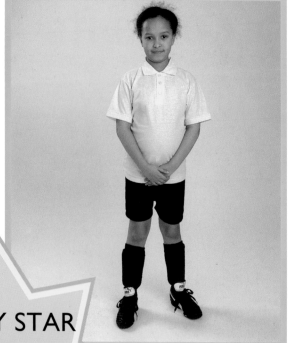

You should also get some **shin pads** to put inside your socks, in case your legs get kicked.

SAFETY STAR
If you play a proper game of football you must wear shin pads.

In colder weather you might need to wear a track-suit or a sweatshirt and some jogging pants.

If you are playing outside on grass you should wear proper football boots. The **studs** help you grip and not fall over!

You can get footballs in different sizes. You can get plastic or leather ones. A smaller ball is probably best for you.

plastic

small (size 4)

leather

large (size 5)

Goalkeepers often wear special gloves. These help you to catch the ball and they protect your hands.

Where do you play?

There are lots of places you can play football, but never play near a road!

You can play outside...

or you can play inside, in somewhere like a gym or a sports hall.

Any safe open space is good for playing football. There may be a park nearby where you can play.

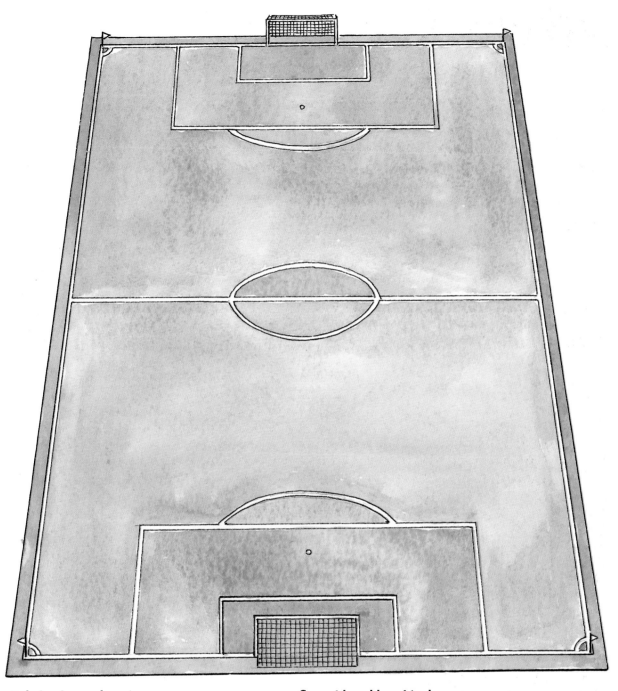

This is what a proper grass football pitch looks like. This is the best place to play.

It is divided up by white lines. It has proper **goal** areas as well.

Are you ready?

Before you play football, make sure your body is ready. This is called a **warm-up**. It helps you to do better, and saves you hurting yourself.

Start with a little run, perhaps around a football pitch.
You can even **dribble** a ball around with you.

SAFETY STAR
Before each football session you must do a proper warm-up.

Now you need to get your **muscles** warmed up. Try some of these **stretching** exercises. They will get your muscles warm and stretchy, so they can move as much as possible.

➤Calf stretch. This stretches the back, lower part of your legs.

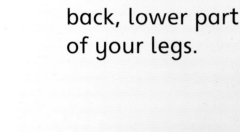

▼Quadricep stretch. This stretches the big muscles at the top, front of your legs.

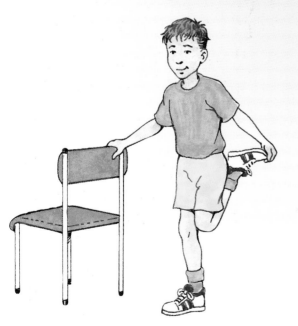

▲Hamstring and lower back stretch. This stretches the top, back of your legs, and your back.

Shall we start?

One way of getting used to a football is to practise catching and throwing it.

Start by bowling the ball along the ground to see how it rolls.

If you have a friend to practise with, roll it to each other. Try picking the ball up in two hands as it comes towards you.

This is what a **goalkeeper** does. They are the only ones who are allowed to use their hands in a game!

Now try a **throw**-in. Use two hands. Flick your body forwards as you throw the ball from above your head.

When you practise with a friend, you can do throw-ins together. You can even practise goalkeepers' catches from the throw-ins.

You can make the throws a bit different by throwing them down. This makes them bounce before they get to your friend.

Can you kick?

Learn to kick the ball properly so you don't hurt your foot. Use the inside of your foot to start with. Never kick with your toes!

keep looking at the ball

use the inside of your foot

follow through with your foot

Start by putting the ball down by your foot. Make sure it is not moving at all before you kick it. Try using both your feet to kick the ball.

For fun, you could find some targets. Cones are good. See if you can hit them with the ball!

If you work with a friend, they can roll the ball towards you. Try using your foot to stop it still. Make sure you are right behind the ball as it comes to you.

When you can stop the ball still, you have learnt to **trap** the ball. This makes it easier to kick the ball away again afterwards.

STAR TIP
Ball control is very important. Remember you won't be able to use your hands in a real game.

Can you pass?

Passing means kicking the ball to someone else.
In a game you pass the ball to your team mates.

To pass you need to practise controlling the ball.
You need to be able to kick it just where you want it.

Practise passing with a friend if you can.

Start off quite close to each other. Don't move further away until you can **trap** and pass the ball properly every time.

SAFETY STAR
Always watch the ball carefully when you are controlling and passing.

To practise on your own, all you
need is a ball and a wall.

Try passing the ball a
long way with a
friend. You might
need to get the ball
up off the ground.
You can do this by
leaning back and
getting your foot
underneath the ball.

Can you dribble?

Dribbling means moving the ball along the ground, with your feet controlling it all the time.

You can use the inside of your foot, the outside, the front, the back or even the bottom!

One of the great things about dribbling is that you can practise it on your own.

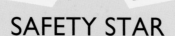

SAFETY STAR
When you are learning to dribble, don't go too fast. Start off by walking. Then get a bit quicker.

When you practise, try going forwards, backwards and sideways. Use all the parts of your foot and both your feet.

Set yourself out a course to dribble around. Cones are good, but you can use stones or clothes to go around.

Dribbling is one of the most important moves in football. It takes a lot of practise to be able to watch where you are going and to dribble around things at the same time!

Let's try shooting!

To **score** a **goal** you have to **shoot**! This is like making a fast **pass**. You have to get the ball into the goal and over the line without the **goalkeeper** saving it.

Kick the ball hard when you shoot. You also have to get it between the goal posts. Practise hitting it into different parts of an empty goal as much as you can.

Remember, you must practise using both feet.

SAFETY STAR
Shooting on target is more important than hitting the ball hard!

It is fun to practise shooting with friends. This is also a chance for you to practise your other football skills. You can pass the ball to each other before you shoot. You can also take it in turns to be the goalkeeper.

If there are enough of you, you can have a game of football. Keep the score and see which team wins!

Use your head!

You are also allowed to use your head for **heading** the ball. But you must be very careful not to hurt yourself when you do a header.

It is a good idea to start off with a balloon or a beach ball.

Remember these rules when you are heading.

1 Only use your forehead – just above your eyes and below your hair.

2 Get underneath and in line with the ball.

3 Always keep your eyes open. Watch the ball all the time.

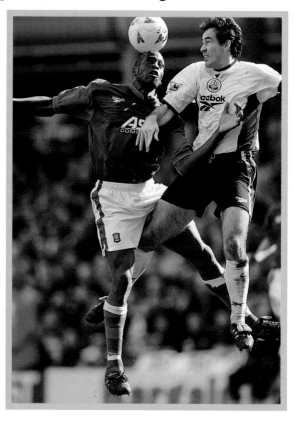

As long as you follow these rules you should not get hurt.

Once you can head a very soft ball, you can start to use an indoor ball. Later try with a plastic ball.

You can practise headers by yourself. Throw the ball up in front of you, then head it back into the air and catch it again.

Try to practise with a friend as well. Gently throw the ball to each other and try to head it back. Remember, do this with light, soft balls first.

If you get really good you may be able to head backwards too!

Playing safe

Rules

These are some of the basic rules of football.

1 Never use your hands to control the ball. Only the **goalkeeper** is allowed to do this.

2 Only **tackle** someone if they have the ball.

3 Don't tackle the goalkeeper.

4 The ball should stay inside the lines of the football pitch during a game.

5 Have a grown-up in charge to make sure everyone plays the game by the rules.

6 Wear **shin pads** to protect your legs.

7 Don't lift your feet too high when you kick, especially if there are others near you.

8 Don't play in dangerous places. Never play near a road.

9 Only kick the ball when you are playing a game or practising. Be careful not to kick each other.

10 The grown-up in charge makes the decisions. Don't argue with them.

Safety

The grown-up in charge should check any equipment you use. If you see anything wrong, tell them!

Equipment should only be moved by grown-ups.

Make sure you are dressed properly for football. If you have boots with **studs**, check they are not sharp.

You must have a proper **warm-up** to get yourself ready.

Cool-down

When you have finished you should have a **cool-down**. This lets your body get back to normal after all the work it has done.

A simple cool-down is to do all of the things you did in your warm-up again. Do fewer of them and for less time.

If you do all of these things then you will enjoy yourself and be safe. Remember,

YOU CAN DO IT!

Glossary

ball control controlling the ball with any part of your body

cool-down exercises you do after a session of sport to relax your body gently

dribble/dribbling moving the ball along the ground using your feet

goal when the ball gets past the goalkeeper and goes over the goal line and into the goal. The team which scores the most goals in a match wins.

goalkeeper player who stays in the goal, stopping goals from being scored and the only player on the pitch allowed to use their hands

header/heading when you use your head to hit the ball

muscle part of your body which helps you bend and stretch

pass/passing giving the football to another player using a kick or header

score when the ball goes into the net a goal is scored

shin pads pads which fit inside your socks to protect the front of your legs

shoot/shooting aiming a kick, or header, at the goal to try to score

stretching moving your muscles at the joints as far as they will go

studs grips which fit on the bottom of football boots to give extra grip on grass pitches

tackle take the ball away from another player

throw-in throwing the ball back onto the pitch after it has gone outside the white lines during a game

trap stop the ball still using your feet

warm-up exercises you do before playing a game to get your body ready

Index